To Isla

The heroine of the story!

Isla Panda and her friends are playing their best-loved game of roly poly.

It is lots of fun and much better than walking.

Down

and down,

round and round they roll.

Bopping into each other

and bouncing off trees and bushes,

Pandas are so fluffy they never get hurt.

Suddenly –

SPLASH

they roll into an unexpected puddle of water. Where has it come from? It hasn't been raining!

As they
shake the
water from
their fur,

Isla can see that
the nearby river
has burst its banks
and she wonders why.

Isla looks downstream and notices that the river is blocked with plastic bottles and other rubbish.

"Oh no!" exclaims Isla "the water can't get through."

"We will have
to remove the rubbish,
or more of the jungle could
be flooded. That would be a
disaster for our friends and
food supply." says Isla.

But how?

Isla looks around
and sees her friend
Tumble is eating
some bamboo...

...and this
gives her
an idea.

Isla asks
Tumble to
chomp down
two long
lengths of
bamboo,

while she tears
off strips from
another piece and
cleverly twists
the strips
into a net.

Working together the friends make an amazing makeshift bridge.

They wonder how to get it across the water.

“I know” says the tallest stretchiest monkey, waggling his floppy hands, “I can swing across!”

Using an extra long vine and taking an extra big leap...

...the monkey swings safely to the other side, landing like an acrobat.

Bit by bit, Isla and her friends push the bamboo bridge across to him. The monkey stretches out his long arms and grabs the bridge, then using some vines he ties the bamboo bridge tightly to a nearby tree.

Isla carefully shimmies out onto the bridge. Being a bear, she's not scared of climbing.

Just as she reaches the middle she loses her grip and starts to slip!

Luckily she manages to
hang on with her strong
legs and sharp claws.
Dangling upside down,
she sees that she is
close to the rubbish
swirling in the water below.

Clinging on to the bridge, Isla
begins scooping up the nasty
rubbish with the net.

The other jungle creatures
all want to help, so
Isla passes the
rubbish filled net to
a monkey...

...who then
gives it to the
red panda...

...who finally hands it to the tiger!

The tiger empties the rubbish into one big pile.
"Why don't we call ourselves the Eco Crew,
as we are doing such a good job."
says the tiger. "That is a great idea."
says Isla.

Finally, the last piece of rubbish is collected…

…and the river runs freely again. HOORAY!

Tumble the red panda asks where the rubbish came from.

Isla explains that instead of recycling it,

some people just throw their rubbish on the ground and a lot of it ends up in rivers and even in the SEA!

"That is terrible," says the red panda.
"We should remind everyone that -
If everybody does their bit
the planet will be fighting fit."

Isla and the Eco Crew stand in front of the big pile of rubbish, happy with doing their bit to help.

The end